For Daniel
from Mrs Gilbertson

For him to keep.

Forces

Graham Peacock

Thomson Learning • New York

Titles in the series:

ASTRONOMY • ELECTRICITY • FORCES
GEOLOGY • HEAT • LIGHT • MATERIALS
METEOROLOGY • SOUND • WATER

First published in the
United States in 1994 by
Thomson Learning
115 Fifth Avenue
New York, NY 10003

First published in Great Britain in 1994 by
Wayland (Publishers) Ltd.

Library of Congress Cataloging-in-Publication Data
Peacock, Graham.
    Forces / Graham Peacock.
        p.   cm. – (Science activities)
    Includes bibliographical references and index.
    ISBN: 1-56847-192-0
    1. Force and Energy – Experiments – Juvenile
literature. 2. Science – Experiments – Juvenile
literature. [1. Force and energy – Experiments.
2. Science – Experiments. 3. Experiments.]
I. Title. III. Series.
QC73.4.P43   1994
531'.078 – dc20   94-16960

Printed in Italy

Acknowledgments
The publishers would like to thank the following for allowing their
pictures to be used in this book: All-Sport (UK) Ltd 13 (inset); Eye
Ubiquitous 18; Science Photo Library *Cover* (left); Tony Stone Worldwide
13 (main); Transport Research Laboratory 14; Zefa Picture Library *cover*
(top right), 23. All commissioned photographs are from the Wayland
Picture Library (Zul Mukhida). All artwork is by Tony de Saulles.

Contents

Words that appear in **bold** are explained in the glossary on page 30.

Gravity

Forces are acting on us all the time. They are the pushes and pulls that affect an object and its movement. The pull of **gravity** keeps our feet on the ground and **friction** stops them from slipping. We use machines to put force where we want it. All movement involves force, from the fall of a feather to the earth circling the sun. This book will help you experiment with forces at home and at school.

Weight

You will need:

◈ a plastic bottle base ◈ a hole punch
◈ a paper clip ◈ a thin rubber band ◈ a ruler
◈ scissors ◈ string ◈ weights ◈ a chair
◈ a large piece of paper ◈ a pen or pencil

1 Make a mass carrier as in the diagram, using the hole punch to make three holes in the bottle base.

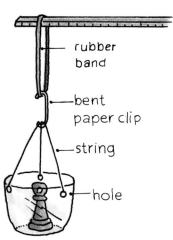

rubber band

bent paper clip

string

hole

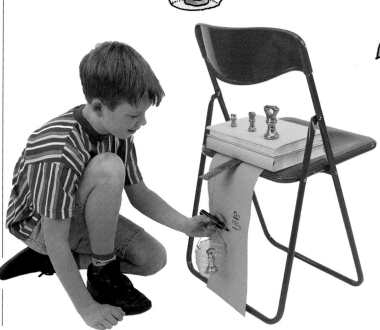

2 Position the paper so that it hangs over the seat of the chair, and place the ruler with the mass carrier over it. Use books to hold it in place.

3 Mark the paper beside the bottom of the mass carrier.

4 Put a 4 oz. weight into the mass carrier and mark the new level on the paper. Add more weight and mark the new level each time.

The greater the **mass** of an object, the greater the pull of gravity on it.

an apple with a mass of 4oz is pulled with a force of 1N

an apple with a mass of 8oz is pulled with a force of 2N

Weight is the downward force of gravity pulling on an object. Scientists measure weight in units called **newtons** (N), named after the scientist Sir Isaac **Newton**.

Do heavy objects fall faster than light ones?

You will need:

◈ 4 or 5 same-size objects of different weights

1 Hold a light object, such as a Ping-Pong ball, in one hand. Hold a fairly heavy object, perhaps a golf ball, in the other hand.

2 Let them go from the same height.

Which hits the ground first?

Or do they hit the ground at the same time?

In the seventeenth century, an Italian scientist named Galileo showed that a heavy cannonball fell at the same rate as a light one. He dropped one of each from the Leaning Tower of Pisa.

Did you know?

If you weigh 600N on Earth you would only weigh 100N on the moon. This is because the moon's gravity is only one-sixth as strong as Earth's.

Air resistance

Why do some objects fall slower than others?

You will need:

◆ 4 or 5 objects of different shapes e.g., a feather, a length of string, a scrap of tissue paper

1 Which of your objects do you think will fall the quickest? Which do you think will fall the slowest? Put them all in order, from the quickest to the slowest.

2 Do a test to see if you are right.

Air resistance slows up very light objects that have a big surface area.

Feather drop

You will need:

◆ a very light, down feather

Drop the feather.

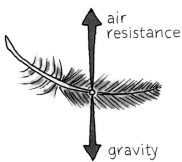

air resistance

gravity

Notice that for most of its drop the feather falls at a constant speed. Air resistance stops it from speeding up as it falls.

Moon drop

On the moon in 1969, American astronaut Neil Armstrong dropped a hammer and a feather at the same time. Even though the feather had a larger surface area, they both landed at the same time.

There is gravity on the moon but there is no air, so there is no air resistance to slow the feather's fall.

Make some air resistance

You will need:
- a sheet of stiff cardboard or a big tray
- a stopwatch or watch with a second hand

1 Hold the cardboard flat in front of you and move it up and down. Is it easy to move through the air?

2 Now hold the cardboard with the edge upward and move it up and down. Why do you think it is easier to move now?

3 Hold the cardboard in front of you and run fast. Can you feel the air slowing you down? The board is adding extra air resistance to your body.

4 Get a friend to time you running with and without the extra air resistance of the board. Make the test fair by running the same distance each time.

Big trucks have to push a lot of air out of the way. This means they have to use more effort to go faster.

Sports cars are specially shaped to allow them to slip through the air easily. This shape is said to be **streamlined**.

Parachutes

Warning! Be careful with plastic bags. Ask an adult to help.

You will need:
◆ plastic bags ◆ thread or thin string
◆ paper clips to act as weights ◆ scissors

Find out:

Which of these shapes makes the best parachute? Cut plastic bags into these shapes, using the same amount of plastic for each.

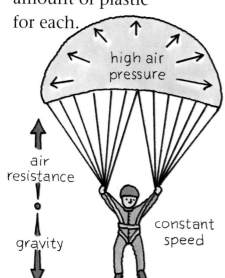

Parachutes fall slowly because of air resistance. The air caught inside the parachute pushes upward, opposite to the force of gravity.

1 Cut a 12-inch square from a plastic bag.

2 Tie equal lengths of string to the corners.

3 Tie all the lengths of string together. Add two or three paper clips.

4 Drop the parachute from up high.

Which is the best material for a parachute?

You will need:

- plastic bags ◈ a sheer curtain ◈ fabric
- different kinds of paper (such as wax paper, construction paper, tissue paper, etc.) ◈ string
- paper clips to act as weights ◈ scissors

1 Make parachutes from different materials. Make the test fair by making them all the same shape and size.

2 Test the parachutes, making a list of their falling speeds. Which material makes the best parachute and why?

Find out:

Does a small hole in the top of the parachute change the way it falls? What happens if you make the hole larger?

Did you know?

In 1960 an American jumped out of a balloon over 18 miles above the ground. He fell 16 miles before opening his parachute.

16 miles

2 miles

Terminal velocity

When the forces of gravity and air resistance are equal, the parachute has reached its **terminal velocity**. This means it doesn't go any quicker as it falls.

Gyrocopters and gliders

A gyrocopter is a helicopter with unpowered rotors.

You will need:

◆ a sheet of paper
◆ scissors ◆ 5 paper clips

1 Cut out a shape as in the diagram.

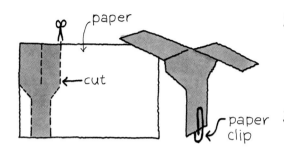

paper

←cut

paper clip

2 Fold the wings and attach a paper clip. You have made a gyrocopter.

3 Hold it up and drop it.

4 Can you make the gyrocopter rotate in the opposite direction?

5 What do you think will happen if you add more paper clips? Try it.

Find out:

What happens if you change the shape of the wings. Is it as good as the original gyrocopter?

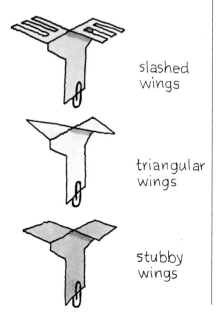

slashed wings

triangular wings

stubby wings

Make a glider

You will need:

◆ a sheet of paper ◆ paper clips

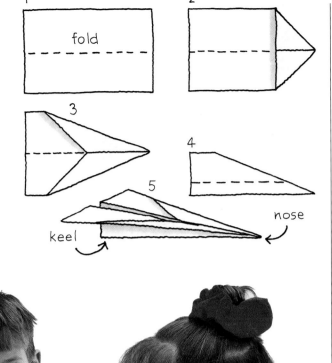

1 Fold the paper following the diagrams shown here.

2 Throw your glider through the air.

3 Add a small paper clip to the nose and compare how it glides.

4 Take the paper clip off the nose and add it to the tail at the back.

Does it glide better with more weight on the front or on the back?

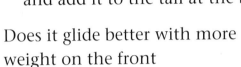

Gliders and gyrocopters get **lift** from the air pushing up under their wings as air resistance. This lift acts in the opposite direction to the pull of gravity.

Did you know?

The longest indoor flight by a paper glider was over 190 feet.

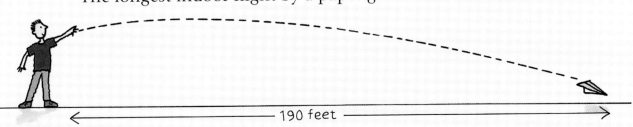

190 feet

Friction

You will need:
- a tray or a sheet of stiff cardboard
- different objects, e.g., an eraser, a matchbox, a plastic cup, a plastic container

1 Put three or four different objects on the tray.

2 Predict which one you think will slip most easily.

3 Slowly lift one end of the tray.

4 Which object moves first?

5 Find out which of all the objects is the most slippery.

Which is the least slippery?

Friction is caused by two surfaces rubbing together. Rough surfaces create more friction than smooth ones. Friction is a force that works in the opposite direction to movement.

Slippery ice

You will need:
- an ice cube ◆ a table

Slide an ice cube along the table surface. A layer of water from the melting ice cube **lubricates** the cube so that there is little friction with the table.

ice cube   water

An ice skater's blade melts the ice because it presses so hard. The blade slides on a layer of water so there is very little friction.

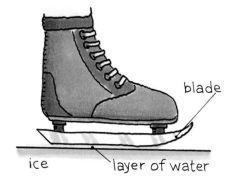

blade

ice   layer of water

What slows a toy car?

You will need:

◆ a toy car ◆ a sheet of wood or stiff cardboard
◆ different surfaces, e.g., carpet, wood, rugs, cloth
◆ books ◆ a tape measure .

1 Make a sloping ramp using the wood and the pile of books.

2 Let the car roll down the ramp onto a smooth floor. How far does it roll?

3 Let it roll onto a carpet. How far does it travel now?

4 Test the car on other surfaces. Which surface has the least friction?

Make the test fair by keeping the slope of the ramp the same in each test.

Slippery shoes

Find out which of your shoes has the best grip.

Do they have the most friction or the least friction?

Do they grip well on all surfaces?

Are they still the best grip on wet surfaces?

Skiers rub wax on their skis to make them slide more easily over the snow.

13

Collisions

You will need:

◈ a toy truck ◈ a plastic container ◈ books
◈ a tape measure ◈ some weights
◈ a sheet of wood or stiff cardboard

1 Set up the ramp using a pile of books under one end. Stand the container at the bottom of it.

2 Let the truck roll down the ramp and hit the container. How far does the container move?

The force of collision depends on the speed and mass of the truck. A fast-moving, heavy truck would hit the container with more force than a slow-moving, light truck.

3 Find out what happens when:

• You add more weight to the truck.

• You raise the height of the top of the ramp.

4 Replace the container with another pile of books and stand the eraser on top of the toy truck.

5 Let it roll down the ramp.

6 What happens to the eraser when the truck hits the pile of books?

The force of collision stops the truck from moving, but the eraser moves on.

The dummies in this test show that if the car stops suddenly in a car crash, the people inside continue to move unless they are held back by a seat belt.

14

Make a catapult

You will need:
- a thick piece of wood (6 in x 4 in)
- a hammer ◆ a thick rubber band
- a plastic spoon ◆ 2 big nails
- modeling clay ◆ a measuring tape

1 Ask an adult to hammer the two nails into the wood, far enough apart so that the elastic band has to stretch to go around both nails.

2 Stretch the elastic band between the two nails.

3 Push the spoon through the band. Turn the spoon, end over end, twisting the elastic band until it is tight.

4 Put pieces of clay on the spoon and hold it down.

5 Making sure that nobody is in the way, fire the catapult by letting go of the spoon.

6 Measure the distances that different-size pieces of clay are thrown by the catapult.

Which size of clay goes the farthest?

The bigger the mass of an object, the larger the force necessary to make it move quickly. You need a very big force to make a large mass move quickly.

In ancient times, battering rams were used to push down doors with a powerful force.

Balancing forces

Why do things fall over?

You will need:
◆ 3 plastic bottles with tops
◆ water ◆ a tray

1 Half-fill the first bottle. Fill the second bottle two-thirds full. Screw the tops on tightly. Keep the third bottle empty.

2 Use your ramp to find out which bottle falls over most easily.

Every object has a **center of gravity**. This is the balance point of an object that determines how **stable** the object is. The bottle with a low center of gravity is more stable than the bottle with a high center of gravity.

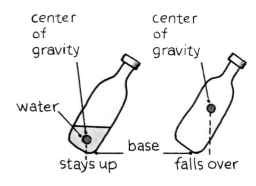

center of gravity

center of gravity

water

base

stays up

falls over

The bottle falls over when the center of gravity is outside the base of the bottle.

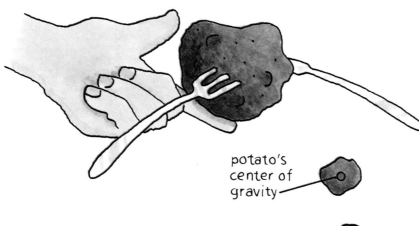

potato's center of gravity

center of gravity of potato and forks

Can you balance a potato?

You will need:
◆ a potato ◆ 2 forks

1 Try to balance a potato on one finger. Impossible?

2 Push two forks into the potato. Easy!

Where is the new center of gravity?

Can you make a balancing clown?

You will need:

◆ stiff cardboard ◆ tape ◆ wire (about 2 feet)
◆ modeling clay ◆ scissors ◆ 2 chairs ◆ string

1 Cut a clown shape from stiff cardboard as in the diagram below.

2 Tape some wire across the back of the clown from one hand to the other, letting it extend as in the picture.

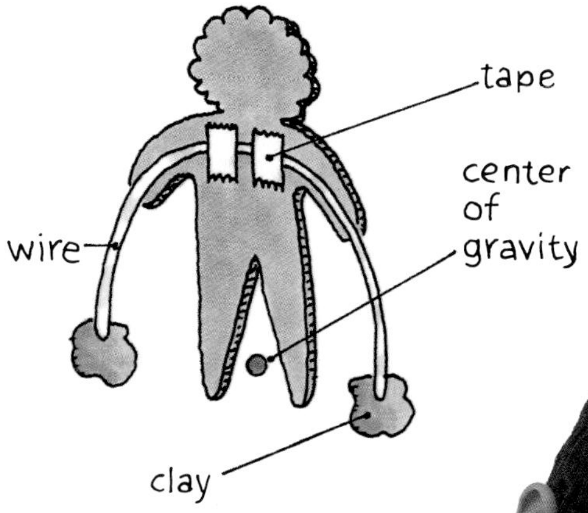

tape

center
of
gravity

wire

clay

3 Attach balls of clay to the ends of the wire.

4 Tie some string between two chairs to make a tightrope. Can the clown balance?

The clown balances if its center of gravity is low enough. What can you do to the clown to make it balance better?

You could use the same method to make a balancing parrot or elephant.

Structures

Making a strong structure

You will need:

- cardboard strips about 2 in x 5 in
- scissors ◆ a stapler ◆ a ruler ◆ weights
- a gap of about 20 in between 2 surfaces
- tape

1 Fold the cardboard strips along the center lengthwise. (It is easier if you score the line with the back of the closed scissors. Guide the scissors with a ruler.)

2 Make a bridge across the gap by stapling the cardboard strips together. Staple them end to end and at right angles to each other to make a bridge framework. Stick the edges of the strips together with tape. Do not fix the bridge to the surfaces in any way —it must just rest on top.

3 What is the biggest weight your bridge can carry? Test it.

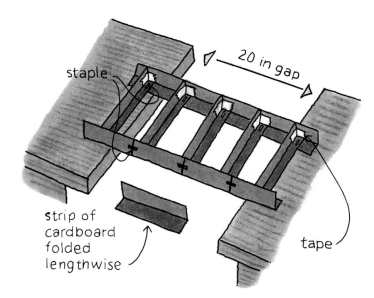

staple

20 in gap

strip of cardboard folded lengthwise

tape

Forces in a structure

You will need

- a sponge
- a felt-tip pen

1 Draw lines on the sponge with the felt-tip pen.

2 Bend it.
Notice that the lines are squashed at the bottom and stretched at the top.

Even long objects that seem stiff, such as girders and beams, bend in a similar way to the sponge.

Girders are used in the construction of buildings and bridges. They are shaped pieces of metal that are stiffer than flat sheets.

What size tube is the strongest?

You will need:

- 2 chairs weighted by heavy books
- 6 sheets of paper ◆ a hole punch
- string ◆ a plastic bottle base
- a ruler ◆ tape ◆ weights

1 Make a mass carrier as described on page 4.

2 Roll one of the sheets of paper very tightly so that it is like a rod and hold it together with tape.

3 Roll the other sheets to make tubes of different **diameters**.

4 Balance each tube between the two chairs with the mass carrier hanging from it. Place different weights in the carrier to find out which diameter of paper tube is the strongest.

Make a mass carrier as described on page 4.

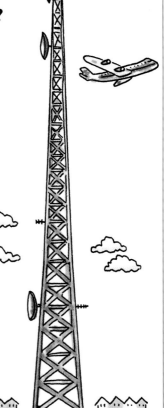

Did you know?

The tallest structure in the world used to be the Warszawa radio mast in Poland. It was 1,940 feet tall before it fell in 1991.

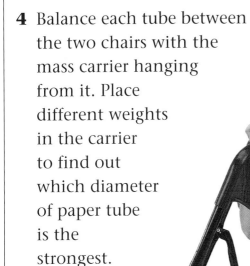

Levers and gears

Experiment with levers

You will need:

◆ a pencil ◆ tape ◆ a small box
◆ a ruler ◆ 6 coins the same size

1 Attach the pencil to the box with tape.

2 Balance a ruler on the pencil.

3 Put one coin 4 inches from the middle of the ruler.

4 Where do you need to place two coins on top of each other to make the ruler balance?

5 Move the single coin closer to the center or **pivot**. Record the distance.

6 Where do you need to put three coins to balance the ruler?

Can you work out a way of predicting where to place the coins in order to balance the ruler?

A light person can balance a heavier person by sitting farther from the pivot.

pivot

hinge

Door lever

You will need:

◆ a door

1 Ask an adult to try to open the door by pushing near the hinge.

2 Now open the door yourself by pushing near the handle. Easy?

The farther you are from the pivot of the door, the easier it is to move it.

How do bicycle gears work?

You will need:

◆ a bicycle with at least 5 gears ◆ a piece of chalk ◆ a long ruler or tape measure

1 Put the bicycle into low gear. Make a chalk mark on the ground next to the front wheel.

2 How far does the bicycle travel with one turn of the pedals?

3 Put the bicycle into high gear. Start it next to the chalk mark again.

4 How far does it travel with one turn of the pedals now?

Bicycles use pedals as levers to turn the chain wheel. What other levers can you find on the bicycle?

Low gear

This is used to climb hills. It is very slow on flat ground.

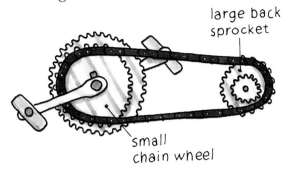

large back sprocket

small chain wheel

High gear

This gear is best for going fast downhill or fast on flat ground. It is very difficult to climb steep hills in top gear.

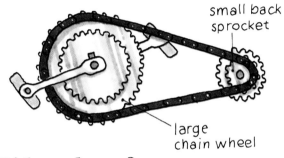

small back sprocket

large chain wheel

Did you know?

The big wheel on the old-fashioned bicycle meant that it went a long way with one turn of the pedal.

distance traveled for each wheel turn

Swinging and spinning

Make a pendulum

You will need:

◆ a ruler ◆ a length of string ◆ heavy books
◆ a stopwatch or watch with a second hand
◆ modeling clay or a ball

1 Place the ruler so part of it extends off a table. Use books to hold it in place. Tie the string to the ruler.

2 Fix some clay or a ball to the end of the string and let it swing.

3 Time how long it takes for your **pendulum** to swing ten times.

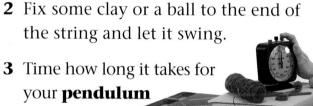

Find out:

• Does adding more clay make the pendulum swing faster?

• Does changing the length of the string make the pendulum swing faster?

Challenge

Can you make a pendulum that swings once every second?

Double and triple pendulums

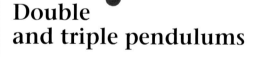

You will need:

◆ 2 chairs ◆ string ◆ 3 pendulums

1 Tie a slack string between two chairs.

2 Tie two pendulums to the string.

3 Swing one of the pendulums. What happens to the other one?

4 Tie three pendulums to the string.

What do you think will happen when you make one of them swing?

Can you make a spinner?

You will need:

◆ cardboard ◆ a compass ◆ a long pencil
◆ a short pencil ◆ modeling clay ◆ scissors

1 Use the compass to draw a circle on the cardboard. Cut out the circle.

2 Push a pencil through the middle of the circle. Spin the pencil.

3 Find out how to make it spin better.

You could:

• Change the length of the pencil.

• Add some clay weights.

• Change the size of the circle.

A spinner with a low center of gravity is more stable than one with weight higher up. Spinners that are well-balanced spin for longer than those where the weight is on one side.

Put a drop of water near the center of the spinner.

Spin the spinner.

What happens to the water?

Spinning forces push the riders outward on this amusement park ride.

Sprinkler

You will need:

◆ a plastic pot with holes in it ◆ string
◆ a wet cloth

1 Hang the pot from the string.

2 Twist the string around and around.

3 Put the wet cloth into the pot. Let the string unwind. What happens to the water?

23

Floating and sinking

You will need:

◆ 3 or 4 fist-sized rocks ◆ rubber bands
◆ a deep bowl of water
◆ a spring balance scale

1 Place a rubber band around each piece of rock.

2 Weigh each rock using the spring balance.

3 Now immerse each rock in water and weigh again.

4 How much weight does each rock lose?

Volume

You can find out the **volume** of a rock by seeing how much water it pushes out of the way (**displaces**).

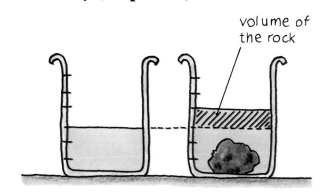

volume of the rock

Find out:

Is there a connection between the weight lost by a rock in water and its volume?

Floating forces

You will need:

◆ a small collection of objects that float
◆ 2 clear containers of water ◆ 2 straws
◆ 3 handfuls of salt ◆ 4 paper clips ◆ a spoon

1 Add three handfuls of salt to one of the containers of water and stir it until the salt dissolves and the water becomes clear.

2 Float identical objects in each container at the same time.

3 Look carefully and compare how well each object floats. What do you notice?

Make a floater

1 Attach two paper clips to the bottom of each straw to make two floaters.

2 Put a floater in each container and compare the level that each floats in the water.

What is the difference in height between the two floaters?

Because salt water is heavier than fresh water, the floater does not push away (displace) as much salt water. This means it floats higher.

Plimsoll mark

The Plimsoll mark is used to show the level to which ships can be loaded and still float safely. A loaded ship will float higher in salt water than in fresh water.

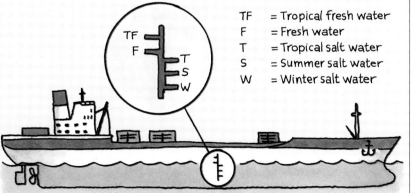

TF = Tropical fresh water
F = Fresh water
T = Tropical salt water
S = Summer salt water
W = Winter salt water

Magnetic force

Magnetism is a force like gravity. It can affect things at a distance, and the magnet doesn't need to touch the object.

Label the walls of your room using the directions from the compass.

The earth is a magnet

You will need:

◆ a bar magnet ◆ a big bowl of water
◆ a deep plastic dish ◆ a magnetic compass

1 Float the dish in the bowl of water. Put the magnet on the dish.

2 Wait until the dish and magnet have stopped turning.

3 Which direction does the north (red) **pole** point in?

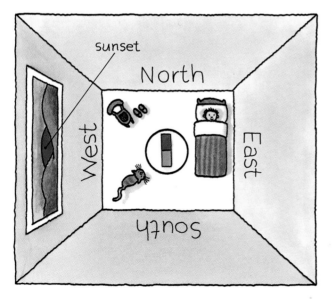

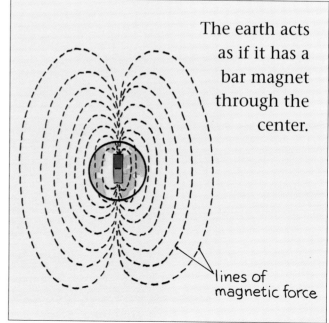

The earth acts as if it has a bar magnet through the center.

lines of magnetic force

Attraction and repulsion

You will need:

◆ 2 bar magnets ◆ a big bowl of water
◆ a deep plastic dish ◆ an iron nail

1 Put one magnet in the dish and float the dish in the water. Wait until the floating magnet becomes still.

2 Now bring the north pole of the second magnet close to the north pole of the floating magnet. What happens?

3 Move the south pole of the second magnet near the north pole of the floating magnet. What happens now?

4 Bring the iron nail near the north pole of the magnet. Now bring it near the south pole. Is there any difference?

Force field

You will need:

◆ a bar magnet ◆ a transparent container filled with iron filings

1 Put the container of iron filings on top of the bar magnet, between the north and south poles.

2 Gently tap the container.

3 Draw the patterns you see.

• Where are the filings lying flat?

• Where are they standing up a little?

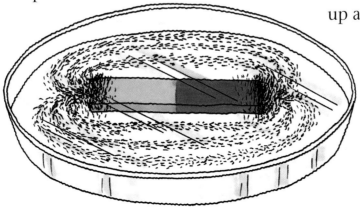

Making magnets

You will need:

◆ 2 large needles ◆ a thimble ◆ a cork
◆ a strong magnet ◆ tape
◆ a small piece of cardboard

1 Using the thimble, gently push one of the needles into the cork.

2 Stroke the other needle with one end of a magnet in one direction. Do this twenty times.

3 Fold the cardboard lengthwise and tape the magnetized needle to it. Balance the cardboard on the cork and needle. Use it like a compass.

4 What happens when you bring one end of a magnet near it?

Make a screwdriver magnet

You will need:

◆ a screwdriver ◆ a magnet ◆ tiny nails

1 Stroke the screwdriver five times in one direction with the magnet.

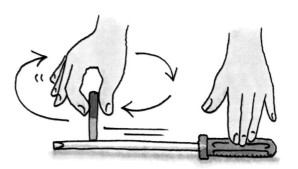

How many tiny nails will it pick up?

2 Do you think it will pick up more nails if you stroke it longer?

Test this idea.

Did you know?

You can spoil a magnet by dropping it or hitting it.

Try this with your needle or screwdriver magnet.

28

How strong is your magnet?

You will need:

◆ 3 or 4 magnets ◆ paper clips ◆ thin string or thread ◆ a ruler ◆ the bottom of a plastic bottle ◆ a hole punch ◆ coins ◆ a rubber band

1 Make a mass carrier as described on page 4.

2 Hang the paper clip from the magnet and use this to test your magnet, adding coins as weights.

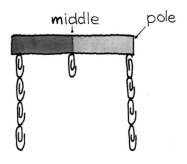

3 Does a magnet have the same strength all over? Test one by picking up paper clips as in the diagram above.

Magnetism is strongest at the poles of the magnet and weakest in the middle.

True or false?

1 You would weigh less on the moon than you do on the earth.
2 Air resistance slows the fall of a parachute.
3 On the moon a hammer falls faster than a feather.
4 A small force can make a large mass move a great distance.
5 An unstable object has a high center of gravity.
6 Objects float better in fresh water than in salt water.
7 The Plimsoll mark has six levels marked on it.
8 Bricks weigh less in water than in the air.
9 In top gear on a bike, you can go up steep hills more easily.

The answers are on page 32.

Glossary

Air resistance The force with which air opposes the movement of an object through it. The faster the object moves, the greater the air resistance.

Center of gravity The balance point of an object; that is, the point where gravity acts upon an object.

Diameter A straight line through the center of a circle.

Displaces Pushes out of the way. An object that floats in water displaces the water.

Force A pull or a push.

Friction A force that happens when two surfaces rub against each other. Friction always opposes movement.

Gravity Every object with mass exerts a gravitational pull. Earth, having a huge mass, has a huge gravitational pull. This force of attraction is gravity.

Lift The upward force of air which is at right angles to the wind and enables airplanes and gliders to resist the force of gravity.

Lubricates Helps something slide. Reduces friction.

Mass The amount of matter an object is made up of. It is measured in grams.

Newton Sir Isaac Newton (1642–1727) was an English scientist who studied motion and forces.

Newtons (N) The measure of force. Weight is measured in Newtons (N).

Pendulum A long weighted object that swings backward and forward. The rate of swing depends on its length.

Pivot Also called the fulcrum. The center point upon which anything turns or depends. A lever acts upon the pivot.

Poles The ends of a magnet. Magnetic force is concentrated at the poles.

Stable Unlikely to fall over.

Streamlined Able to slip easily through the air with little air resistance.

Terminal velocity The final speed of a falling object. A feather has a low terminal velocity but a stone will have a high terminal velocity. It is the speed reached when the force of air resistance equals the force of gravity.

Volume The amount of space an object occupies.

Weight The force with which gravity pulls a mass.

Books to read

Dunn, Andrew. *Lifting by Levers*. How Things Work. New York: Thomson Learning, 1993.

Dunn, Andrew. *Simple Slopes*. How Things Work. New York: Thomson Learning, 1993.

Friedhoffer, Robert. *Forces, Motion, and Energy*. Scientific Magic. New York: Franklin Watts, 1992.

Morgan, Sally and Morgan, Adrian. *Movement*. New York: Facts on File, 1993.

Nardo, Don. *Gravity: The Universal Force*. San Diego: Lucent Books, 1990.

Spurgeon, Richard. *Energy and Power*. Tulsa, OK: EDC Publishing, 1993.

Taylor, Barbara. *Weight and Balance*. Science Starters. New York: Franklin Watts, 1990.

Wellington, Jerry. *The Super Science Book of Forces*. Super Science. New York: Thomson Learning, 1994.

Chapter notes

Pages 4–5 Mass and weight are two different quantities. Mass is measured in grams. It is a measure of the amount of matter. Weight is the force that gravity exerts on a mass. So on the moon, where gravity is less, an object weighs less. Unless air resistance is very great, heavy objects and light objects fall at the same rate.

Pages 6–7 In the "feather drop" activity, notice that in your hand the feather is still. When you let it go, it must accelerate then continue to fall at a constant speed. At this point the feather is neither speeding up nor slowing down, so it has reached its terminal velocity. Where there is no air to get in the way, as on the moon, there is no such thing as terminal velocity. Even a feather will keep going faster and faster until it hits the surface of the moon.

Pages 8–9 When testing the different shapes of a parachute, you will be testing roughly equal areas. The hole in the parachute will probably make it fall slower since it stabilizes the fall and stops the parachute rocking from side to side.

Pages 10–11 Sycamore and ash seeds drop in much the same way as the gyrocopter. To make the gyrocopter rotate in the opposite direction simply reverse the wings.

Pages 12–13 The ice skater's blade melts the ice through pressure. This has nothing to do with friction producing heat.

Pages 14–15 A large mass moving slowly will produce a big force in a collision. A small mass, like a bullet traveling at 500 mph, will also exert a lot of force when it hits something. The mangonel was an ancient siege machine weapon that was used to fire rocks at castle walls. It will fire a small mass farther than it will fire a large mass. You may have to slide the rubber bands up the nails to allow you to twist them and the spoon.

Pages 16–17 The potato's center of mass is approximately in its middle but when you add forks to it the center of mass is below the finger on which it is balancing so it cannot topple.

Pages 18–19 Don't use thick cardboard which may be too strong for these tests. When you bend the sponge, notice that the sponge at the top is stretched. This sponge will pull against your stretching force. The sponge at the bottom pushes against your squashing force. This is how structures stay up. The material of the structure is squashed and stretched and this equals the pushing and pulling forces of things such as wind and gravity.

Pages 20-21 To work out the turning forces on a simple lever you multiply the distance from the pivot by the mass. For instance, a mass of 5 g which is 6 cm from the pivot has a turning force of 30. The penny farthing bike was an early attempt to speed up bikes. Before this, bikes used pedals to turn the front wheel directly and were very slow along the flat.

Pages 22-23 The swing of a pendulum depends exclusively on its length. Old clocks used a pendulum as a way of keeping a regular beat. Musical metronomes are simply stiff, upside-down pendulums. Objects on a spinning surface fly outward unless stopped from doing so by another force such as the pull exerted by a piece of string.

Pages 24–25 Objects float when they displace a weight of water equal to their own weight. Objects which float have a density less than that of water. Water has density of 1 g/cm3. (In other words each cubic centimeter has a mass of 1 g.) Objects which sink have density greater than 1 gram per cm3. They displace less than their own weight of water.

Pages 26–27 You may wonder why the north magnetic pole of the earth attracts the north pole of your magnet. To do this, there must be a south magnetic pole at the north pole! Magnetic reversals happen fairly frequently in geological terms and have many applications in earth science since they give information about the position and age of rocks which have magnetic particles in them. Always put iron filings in a sealed container.

Pages 28–29 When you make a magnet using an existing one, you don't reduce the magnetism of the original. All the energy comes from the movement of your hand. When you stroke a steel needle, you are aligning the tiny molecules, or groups of molecules in the steel which are normally arranged randomly. Notice how little weight the magnet can hold at its center.

Index

Answers to questions on page 29:
1 True, **2** True, **3** False, **4** False, **5** True, **6** False, **7** False, **8** True, **9** False